The World Book

THE WORLD BOOK

Poems by

Steven Cramer

Copper Beech Press

Thanks are due the editors of the periodicals in which some of these poems, or earlier versions of them, originally appeared: *AGNI* ("The Marriage of Heaven and Hell," "1963," "What We Didn't Risk"), *The Antioch Review* ("Eclogue"), *The Atlantic* ("The Accident"), *Boulevard* ("Constellations," "The Feeder," "His Wish"), *The Graham House Review* ("A Sudden Change in Temperature," "The World Book"), *Indiana Review* ("After the Miracle," "Creosote," "First Kiss"), *New England Review/Bread Loaf Quarterly* ("The Haircut"), *The New Republic* ("The Storyline"), *The North American Review* ("The Black Minus"), *The Paris Review* ("Jacuzzi," "Nocturne"), *Partisan Review* ("After Bypass"), *Ploughshares* ("Mother Conjuring in Hondo, Texas: 1945"), *Poetry* ("The Battle of the Bands," "For the Bullies of West Morris High," "The Game," "The Hospitals"), *Prairie Schooner* ("Hibiscus," "Truce"), and *Tar River Poetry* ("From the Corner of His Eye," "The Parade, 1968").

Lines ten and eleven of "The Black Minus" were adapted from Robert Fitzgerald's translation of *The Odyssey,* Book II, lines 157-159.

Cover: Joseph Cornell, *An Analemma, Shewing by Inspection the Time of Sun Rising and Sun Setting, the Length of Days and Nights*, 1948-50. Box construction, 15½x20¼x4 in. Copyright © The Joseph and Robert Cornell Memorial Foundation. Courtesy of The Pace Gallery. Photograph by Bill Jacobson Studio.

For information, address the publisher:
Copper Beech Press
English Department
Box 1852
Brown University
Providence, Rhode Island 02912

Library of Congress Cataloging-in-Publication Data
Cramer, Steven, 1953-
The world book : poems / by Steven Cramer. — 1st ed.
p. cm.
ISBN 0-914278-59-2 (pbk. : alk. paper) : $9.95
I. Title.
PS3553.R2676W6 1992
811′.54 — dc20
92-6797
CIP

First Edition
Printed in the United States of America

For Hilary
and in memory of my father (1917-1987)
and my brother (1945-1990)

Finally, the ones carried off too soon no longer need us,
They are weaned from earthly things as gently
As children outgrow a mother's breast. But we who crave
Such great secrets, we whose grievings so often
Give rise to a blessed progress — could we exist without them?

Rilke

CONTENTS

I

THE STORYLINE

is eventful and dreadful, a narrative
Of everyone alive who now is not.
One after another, I knew them all,
I heard those metal drawers clank shut.

The heart's a deadbolt locking in and out.
It catches every time the dying starts.
The chest expands around it, a furnace
Surging and flaring with what — with guilt?

Of course, of course, it's natural,
Near the end of the plot, to number
And shun the dead. After the flicker
Of lament, after the traces of paradise

In their silver urns, after their spirits
Hover near enough to chime *not yet, not yet, now,*
You'd think it's nothing to take their hands.
You'd think, with either fear or praise,

You'd know the single way to enter
Such cold water: lastborn of the family, only
Surviving son, one death in front of another,
Step into this undertow, without risk.

JACUZZI

Chlorine and languor and vaporous
Threads rising like the steam off soup,
This brackish whirlpool wrinkles us
And turns us briefly old until our time
Runs out: twenty minutes at the most.
But it's nothing like that girl
Who heated me to my fingernails
As we slow-danced on a lantern-lit patio,
My palms so moist she squealed
And whispered to her friends,
While my face burned faintly, blue.
Twelve of us, strangers, ring the tub.
Like those early surgeons who bled
The sick, we're convinced sweat heals,
And loitering in these eddying pools,
Buoyed by the undercurrents, flushes out
The mortal downrush coursing through us.
So that day a new guest waded in —
A man so thin, so undone,
He looked like a trembling aspen
In a flood — we all looked, at a loss,
Then looked away, scanning our hands
For paper cuts, for sores, torn nails,
Any breach in the skin, through which
The idea of such illness could get in.
No one found the nerve to speak or leave
When the time came. After he waded out,
Trunks clinging to his hips like drenched
Newsprint, we stayed in long enough
For him to shower, dry off, dress.
While the water swirled around us,
I heard that August breeze
Disquieting the paper lanterns,
Carrying those girlish whispers back.

WALKING ON THE CEILING

with my sister

Like me, do you remember it as easy?
Easy as borrowing Mother's hand mirrors —
Mine with its hairline crack, yours
With a handle ivory-white and sharp.

Holding them face up, under our noses,
We turned ceiling into floor and leapt
Over the transoms looming in each doorway,
Kitchen light-coils hissing at our feet.

Soon we'd learn to walk right through
The diningroom chandelier's glass corolla,
And skirting the TV room, with its oceanic
Surges of canned laughter or "Ed Sullivan,"

We examined the molding's blistered paint
Like the marbled skin a man once thrust at us
Along with a warning about cherrybombs,
His three remaining fingers gnarled

Into a cypress root, that hideous trophy
Father brought home from his hole-in-one.
Remember how it pointed from the high shelf
In the den? Remember the delirium of stairwells,

Chains alert as charmed snakes? Remember
How we'd separate? Suddenly grown bored,
As if you'd woken to the year between us,
You'd escape to the room you barred me from,

And I'd stalk back to Mother's bathroom, sick
Of our upended world, and aim my mirror
At its double hanging over her vanity
And linger a moment in infinity.

THE GAME

I'm Dead, my family named it. "Someone
Will be crying soon," my mother warned,
Those summer nights I'd beat him with my fists
Until he dropped, groaned with a last breath
"I'm dead," and expired operatically,
A death scene straight out of *The Three Stooges.*

Our bedeviled collie looking on, I'd run —
Impressed, ecstatic — a fright almost erotic
Zinging up my spine as the back stairs
Creaked behind me and, returned to life,
My older brother filled my bedroom door.
That's how I learned the soul lives after death

(Even though, among us, it's an article
Of faith that it does not). It flares and chars
Like lit tissue; or implodes, a white dwarf
Slowly cooling inward, then nothing;
Or because we all were reared on television,
It's the silver iris collapsing in the screen.

So when my brother, dead at forty-five,
Was discovered on his bathroom floor,
A hair dryer gunning heat across the tiles,
Believing the nothing we believe,
None of us would have him rise above
The graduation photos, candids with guitar,

All ranked along a marble tabletop —
Each frame is a tangible we handle.
The mystery that frustrates us is the love
Required of survivors, the invisible
Grace to press against what terrifies
And restores — like the scent, adolescent,

Medicinal, as I buried my face in his neck,
Pounding, pounding his shoulders and back,
Until his lovely cartoon kick of death.
And after this, his body, inert at first,
Stirs into our game of resurrection, the dog
Above him, moaning, believing what it sees.

HIS WISH

Finally my brother got his wish —
Music with no distortion. Most of his life
He'd suffered the crackle of static
When a needle settled onto vinyl;
The surface hiss of a cassette
Could make him weep. Listening
Became a kind of agony,
The invention of the compact disc
A visitation of grace. After the funeral,
His widow leads us — sister,
Brother, sister — into his music room;
Tells us to play any disc we wish. Earlier,
Because we hate her
For surviving him, especially
When she cries, our lips
Brushed against her cheek
Like paper against paper. Now
The black components of his stereo
Flutter and blink, and it's true:
From the grill of his speakers,
The Ravel we treat ourselves to
Comes through exquisitely, pure,
Unspoiled by touch.

CREOSOTE

Acid stink of blackened jetties
Sloping to the breakers, sectioning the beach
Into *Guarded Area* or *Swim at Your Own Risk*,
Its dark preservative applies
To everything off-limits, over my head:
The tarred pilings, their spirals of oil;
The stinging odor of the train depot,
Railroad ties choked with beheaded dolls;
But worst of all it recalls that kid
Who blistered my face into the noon sand
Until his father grabbed his hair, yanked him
Off my back and dragged him home. Three decades
Later, convinced I've become immune,
I pass a worksite where it's laid on thick,
A soured cloud of memory drifting back:
One-season towns with names like *Sea Girt*
Or *Beach Haven*; inside their cold-water bungalows
The midnight accusations, drunken cries, the crack
Of slapped flesh escaping through the screens,
The heat that made us one cruel family. That kid
Grew more poisonous than anything I'd known
And more deliberate. All summer he brooded
Around the cottages, a constant threat of ambush,
Until I found a brief hiding place
Where the boulders rose sharply from the surf,
Ballasting the creosoted jetty wall.
High tides dug out a network of grottoes,
Shifting caves where I could catch my breath.
So when the men discovered a boy too late,
His foot trapped between swollen wood and rock,
Ankle razor-shredded by the barnacles,
You can bet whose body I saw fastened there,
Whose salt-encrusted face they veiled with tarp;
And returning later to the site, I breathed in deep
That lethal and medicinal creosote,
Trusting in this punishment more permanent
Than any I could devise, and more kind.

THE HAIRCUT

At thirteen what I hated most
Was not the aftermath of slicked-
Down stickiness, nor the barber's
Wet breath misting on my ear,
The sting as his scissors
Nipped cartilage or lobe;
And not the fuming barbicides
In formation like prohibition
Booze, the faced-off mirrors
Doubling the damage done
To duck's ass, Beatle bangs,
Curlicues descending from
The temples to dissemble
As sideburns . . .

With a hiss
My mother buzzed her palm
From nape to crown, following
Her orders to spot-check
Each half inch cropped.
Drafted to cast her lot
Against my flowering anima,
She watched my bristling
Scalp as I glowered home,
Placing a city block between us,
Sweating to outgrow that skirt-
Clinging youngest son
Undone without his camouflage.

Even after the glancing
Jolt of the shop windows,
My head unbearably shrunken,
As if I'd held my nose, ears,
And mouth and sucked in hard;
Even after I showered off
The fallout and blow-dried

The stubble nibbling my neck,
The worst came down at dinner
In the weight of Father's hand
Kneading my bare shoulders,
And my home-grown estrangements
Clipped to a truth I hated to admit:
Shorn like that it *was* a shock
How much we looked alike.

II

1963

isn't just a memory of your breasts,
Mrs. Monroe. Unmotherly and wide-set
Under the sheer synthetic of your blouse,
They snowed chalk as you bent to check our math.
At recess we pondered their ampleness,
Nicknamed you "Marilyn" behind your back.
But your smoke-toughened voice was pure Bacall.

Were love and death beyond the likes of us?
Our fifth-grade laps tingled as you strode
Between the rows, our callow ideal of glamour.
When you barked instructions, a siren crying wolf,
We "ducked-and-covered" underneath our desks,
Still managing to cop looks up your dress
Until "All Clear." The only married teacher

In that elementary school of nunnish thugs,
You pulled your anger tight, smirked to soften it.
Like Bernstein you'd conduct the Palmer Method
While we inscribed our names across the air.
And out from under the chalkboard's cirrus dust,
The ghost of Lincoln arrowed straight to King
In cloudy night-class parallels you left

For us to riddle out. But what you failed,
Or weren't allowed, to teach us I remember
Best: when the Principal came beckoning
At the classroom door, and everywhere else
News broadcasts made the world go weightless,
You marched back from the hall without a hint,
Turning our heads instead to the stone gods

From *National Geographic,* pitfalls of diphthongs
In our spelling books, until the last bell
Dismissed us to face our weeping elders.
After this you vanish, imperfectly
Dispersed into a history half-withheld,
Leaving a nimbus of bleached hair, a scumbled
Penmanship, a blackboard partially erased.

FIRST KISS

He pressed her against the sweating wall
Of South Orange Episcopal Church,
The stone spines denting his palms,
Leaving their impressions to this day,
As I push myself from my desk,
Tired of waiting, tired of wanting
The taste of her, a milky tinge
Leavened with clove gum,
And all this aimless desire
Coming nowhere near close enough.

Useless to wish her back,
To give her a name and parents . . .
It was the end of winter.
They hardly knew to open their mouths
And let their tongues slip through.
He pursed his lips as he'd been taught
To coax sound from a clarinet,
And when she sighed she wanted more,
It was more than enough and more
Than he knew.

                    Oh, he knew
The uses of speechlessness,
For the feeling of needing so much,
I'm cornered and left in that cold
Alcove, clinging to her, somewhere
Between rectory and churchyard.
Sure I could push her harder
Against those stones. The March chill
Would pierce the small of her back.

Or I could walk him home
Afterwards, a new knowledge
Waking in straining ligaments,

And settle him in his single bed,
As if this story continued
When I stopped — no beginning, no middle,
No end in sight; no girl, no kiss
To speak of; and her name was Abby
And our lips chafed and chafed again,
Coming as close as we could.

FOR THE BULLIES OF WEST MORRIS HIGH

Their childhoods had come and gone
In a welter of manure smells and morning fog
And fistfights with their dads, tractor debris
Oiling their unseeded lawns
Like flotsam from destroyers lost at sea.
But this is speculation.

Loitering between classes where the corridor
Curved past a diorama
Of the Parthenon — on each side flanked
By school editions of Euripides, Aeschylus, and Homer —
They backed their dungarees against the glass,
Closed ranks as if to keep us from those myths

They weren't the heroes of.
Or fishing out a longhair from the shower stall,
They'd lather up his head
With hocks until the kid begged shamelessly
To be cast back. Homeroom to gym, shop to study hall,
These hydra-headed farmers' sons held sway.

Something about these Ralphs and Orens,
Dennises and Earls, has quietly turned timeless.
Like shame, the memory of them smolders
Half-hidden in the embers of cupped cigarettes.
On subways now one sometimes reawakens
Briefly in the nasal cough
Behind our backs, that stiffening in our shoulders

Before they flayed our shirts from loop to belt.
If to us they looked like avatars
Of Polyphemus, they weren't killed so easily.
Even those the government had dealt
Unlucky numbers in the Lottery
Would have joined up anyway,
Determined to refuel whatever wars

The likes of us had marched against.
And when one or two showed up each year
Between the hallway's lockered walls
In gauzy graduation photographs
Assembled in that same plate glass display,
Their violent grins, circled by wreaths,
Grew handsome in the afterglow of death.

THE BATTLE OF THE BANDS

for Thom Swiss

Testing, testing, one, two, three
We'd chant into the mike, until we tickled
Up a high-strung squeal that looped and skirled
From speaker to mike to speaker to speaker,
Finally yanking taut inside our ears.
For us the true was never the beautiful.

And we only knew the good by scent,
By the sugary stink of it: the good
Shit we bought in the smallest quantities.
The sparse crowd milled about, like gawkers
At a curbside accident, which we wanted more
Than anything to sound like, driving the music
Toward a burlesque of massacred amps:

Ken chopping lead on his Hendrix-style Strat;
A step ahead on rhythm, his older brother Mike,
Draft-age but so convincingly a lunatic
They'd take a priest before they'd call him up;
Fred thumbing his Fender bass, adorably saurian
In thigh-tight Naugahyde; while I'm behind
A drumset gaudy as a float on the Fourth of July,
Its Japanese red glitter and Zildjian cymbals

International as America, where four thousand like us
In a thousand community clubs and high school gyms
Fought *The Battle of the Bands*, bashing out
Our skeletal covers of "Eight Miles High,"
"Revolution," "Purple Haze," sophomoric vocals
Sputtering through the grill of our P.A.
And if we gigged that Saturday
(March 16, 1968),

While along the bloodied mud roads of My Lai
Purple haze streaked in the flick of a cigarette,
A year would pass before we got the picture
Of the truth; in twenty we'd watch it replayed
As the film's soundtrack of Sixties hits
Fired us all to nostalgia, flashing back
Those battles of the bands we fought and won;
And jammed until midnight, drilling our riffs
Into the dispersing audience.

THE MARRIAGE OF HEAVEN AND HELL

Sticking out our tongues and lapping up
The stamp-sized patch of newsprint with a watermark,
We chewed well, swallowed, and slouched back
To watch the walls for telltale sighs and swellings,
Wide-eyed pupils waiting for the brain gates
To unlatch, our nervous systems
To be colonized, enlightenment
The last thing on our minds. Who cared
About the deities aglow in every windowpane,
Or if this microdot bolt from the blue
Boosted our mystical wattage?
At most we hungered for a hurricane
Lamp kicked over into straw,
A quick blitz of peace. After all,
We called a dose a hit, and on the face of it,
The bliss we longed for smacked
Of the prenatal, the giddiness infiltrating us
Crystallized into glass stilts
From which we saw ourselves take off —
Weightless and iridescent as dragonflies.
That's the kind of lightness I remember
Released the night I last ingested it,
Until it shanghaied me
On a field trip off my head: half the distance
From Brookside to the Mendham VFW.
We turned left, and the road sank into mud,
My foot a centaur's hoof on the accelerator,
Bruce, Jim, and someone nameless with a goatee
Heckling like jackals in the Mustang's backseat,
And all my body parts autonomous.
The shack we drove toward hosted rites
Tribal enough to levitate the President.
When I saw music oozing out the windows
So palpably I thought the house coughed blood,
I waded upstream, toward a shadow dance

Branded by the strobe lights on the shades.
Like silhouettes of the vaporized,
They flash back in my wish to taste
The muddy reek of black, or listen
To the rainbow flavor of my own saliva;
A wish to resurrect that shack
And make it stand for something paradisiacal,
Maniacal, about America,
Where everywhere is everywhere else —
From midnight to three I danced,
Watching a girl's nipples ringed by flames;
From three to five, everyone I thought
I knew bloomed with a rash of welts
As if from an Old Testament storm of wrath,
Each repeatedly sneezing into the air
Two great wakes of dust.
For an instant I'd metabolized God's eye!
And from his vantage point, my own skin turned
Hypothetical, as the nameless one
And I withdrew to talk each other down,
Insisting we existed:
I am I am I am I am
Repeated like a chorus, prayer, or axiom
Until the sun rose, a yellow-eyed aftertaste,
And one of us kept lapsing into sense.

WHAT WE DIDN'T RISK

Anybody's life, for one. Anyone
Who'd touched us knew our bodies
Too satiny to hazard mortality.
In a candle-lit procession

We sang we were "fixing to die,"
Paired like children filing into gym —
Our pupils dilated, our irises thin.
War dead hung like blood floaters

In the vitreous humor of our eyes.
Black bands on our olive-green sleeves,
We spat out the brick-sounding *k*
In *Amerika*, born too late to flee

With older boys like Jim, or lop off
Our own baby toes like his cousin,
Or torch two VC like Sagurton,
Uniform tucked where an arm had been.

In one surviving photograph,
Michelle Something and I
Lie face down on a naked mattress,
As if we could see through the earth:

Our hips narrow, no wallets
In our Levis pockets, the gooseneck
Lamp hooded with my neckerchief
To redden our sex. Soon we'll plummet

In a flash of charred seeds and paraffin
Back into the seascape of our retinas.
Then we'll sleep, sure our love-cries
Traveled all the way to Indochina.

THE PARADE, 1968

If-I-had-a-gun-I'd-shoot
The-four-of-you-and-ship-you-out
To-Russia-in-that-thing . . .
That's what the girl fired off
Who snatched our peace leaflets
And shredded them one by one.
A month before, she'd lost
Her brother's forearm to Khesanh,
And no three high school juniors
And a 4-F dropout were about
To take her light-drenched noon
Of praise and dampen it
By hauling a makeshift coffin
With a bathroom mirror for a face
Through the Brookside Independence
Day Parade. Shouldering our barge
Of pasteboard down East Main,
Behind the teams of racing toads,
Over the Dismal Harmony Bridge,
Past the jeering Gustafsons,
The Gibbs, the Tufts — who in a week
Would mail our mothers envelopes
Of dung — and pulling up short
Only if a toad got out of hand,
We trudged on staring straight
At our feet. Then cast adrift
With the floats and majorettes
Into the softball field, finally
We found our sign: *Protest*
Aerosoled on cardboard,
Which is when we stopped
To think *Now what?*
The band soured, came undone;
Sparklers drizzled down; our mirror
Sent July's glare heavenward;

And as the townsfolk circled round
To stare, or sneer, or throw
Wet cheers from the dugout roof,
Our faceless casket, stood on end,
Towered over us and them,
A head or more too tall
To reflect on anyone.

III

THE HOSPITALS

It's the season they take the fathers to hospitals.
Wheeled off half-mown lawns, found in cellar-rank
Family rooms, the fathers are sped to Emergency

Where nobody hopes the body lasts forever,
Least of all the fathers, who hold their peace,
Who've shrunk to fit these astonishingly narrow beds.

And they keep the fathers in the hospitals
As if they'd turned up there like unclaimed luggage,
Never to be shipped to their proper address.

Oh, someday they'll make their ahistorical exits —
But not yet. So we watch them take their turns
For the worse, children wading out too far

Or climbing too tall a tree. Knowing no better,
They'll let us believe they once fed the earth,
That their lives were deliberate as money,

That soon we'll understand what makes them valuable.
Then they float off in smoky wreaths and condense,
Resettling on rooftops in a strange neighborhood;

No matter how we plead they won't climb down.

THE WORLD BOOK

That night he came into my room,
The World Book tucked under his arm
(Volume 5, from *Desert* to *Electron*),

He pointed out the structure of my inner
Ear — the hammer, stirrup, and anvil,
The cross-sectioned spiral of the cochlea;

No matter how he diagrammed the ache,
He couldn't stop its throbbing. Years later
On the renal ward, I've brought in a Walkman

To help him pass the hours in dialysis.
His six quarts of blood have turned
Muddy red inside the yards of coiled tubing,

A tainted stream siphoned around a wheel
And through these artificial guts to surface
Purified. And my fantasy is childish:

I repair his faltering body, restitch the nets
Of capillaries, the membranes of hurt cells,
Or at least turn up an image to explain

What brought us here, one pair among twenty —
The patients becalmed and tethered to machines,
Pulsing shunts burrowed in their chests;

And stationed around them, the relatives,
Some motionless, some pacing, all keeping
Watch. My father's eyes close and tighten

As I hover above him. When he falls
Asleep, it's to a music I can't hear
And for which there is no metaphor.

CONSTELLATIONS

At night from the crickety patio,
All the house lights off,
My father calls his family out —
Wife, two daughters, second son —
For the planes descending,
One by one, to Newark.
From horizon to horizon,
His fingers trace their flightpaths:
Two, three, sometimes four
Remote lights declining in a row.

The more we stare, the more stars
Surface in the crowded heavens.
Old navigator, star charts
Stored in his memory,
He points out Hercules overhead,
Scorpio to the south, the Summer
Triangle of Deneb, Vega, Altair:
His guides through World War II.
What course is he devising now,
On leave from the hospital?

Someone points, too late,
At a shooting star, but he
Explains they're only meteors,
Space debris so infinitesimal
Thousands could fit in his palm.
He lifts his hand to the stars
And sees, perhaps, his own
Flame-out in the upper atmosphere,
A split-second of light
No one's quick enough to share.

ECLOGUE

Of the bruised light before sunrise,
The doors locked, the dog asleep,
The constellations in place:

Orion, Hydra, Gemini —
Was he awake or pacing in his sleep?
Was he in the house? Had he taken the car? —

She only says *I found him downstairs walking.*
Of the flashlight that swept his forehead,
Then caught him full on the face,

His eyes flickering: red, dark red, red —
Is this when you last thought him sane?
Or the morning she discovered him

Speaking into a mirror, to his brother
Missing nearly fifty years since Anzio,
Rising like some twin god out

Of the Tyrrhenian, or talking to some other,
She can't say. *Is it always winter*
Where you are? his profile asked

His profile, then he turned to her
And smiled, her own face tightening,
Trying to remember where she was.

Of course there were signs before that:
The mornings he'd patrol the patio,
Spider flowers risen to his chest;

Or pausing at the border of the lawn,
He'd linger under the chestnut tree,
Head cocked, eyes squinting,

Like a sentry straining to hear
Gunfire beyond the horizon. Then,
Beneath the white light in our kitchen,

We stop talking, as if his face
Rose from the surf, and like a tide
Tugging at her ankles, all my questions

Place her once again between that sunrise
Before and the sunrise after. *Not then*
She answers, and after that, *not then.*

TRUCE

My father wakes up choking. After midnight
The lungs his heartbeat labors to pump clean
Flood to the edge of breath. Before the flashlights
Of the paramedics brush the windowpanes,
His wife sits down beside him on the couch,
Cupped in her palm the nitroglycerine's
Glittering pill uplifted toward his mouth.
It's a routine game: she coaxes; he whines
He can't stomach more of those damn things,
Which make him sicker anyway. One last ruse
He sees through every time but never imagines
Surviving the night without, seals their truce:
In a voice more like a mother's than a wife's,
For me, she pleads. He permits her to save his life.

A SUDDEN CHANGE IN TEMPERATURE

By degrees it's clear —
He's still inside this bedroom and will not
Be dusted out. Clear as the suits in the closet
Waiting in line, their shoulders squared.
Clear as the socks in the top drawer,
Each pair folded on itself.
And don't be afraid, no one's here
To avoid anymore, no one
To wake up or shadow the door.
Nobody lies in this bed or rises
Into a blue bathrobe with stars . . .
Because a man once said so to a child,
The stars are really horses traveling
All the way to Istanbul. And did
It look like everyone had fallen
Asleep, his pillows blurring out of sight,
As he pulled on his socks, his robe,
And tired of waiting, shuddering
From the sudden change in temperature,
He closed his eyes and rose and
Stepped over the threshold?

HIBISCUS

Why of all flowers
Did this one please him most?
Transplanted from his ward,
Fronting the mantel of funeral gifts,
It outshines the widows
On their widow's walk, a brash
Cousin breezed in from the south,
Christened "Rose of China,"
A red blare fracturing
The hum of grief. When his heart
Lapsed and relapsed
And his lungs clamored for breath,
Did he watch its petals
Funnel like the early phonograph
Then flare toward their highest pitch
At evening? Unlike him,
It flaunts a gift for reincarnation,
The blossoms delivered each morning
By nightfall wrinkled sacks,
The arc from birth to death
Collapsed to a single day.
And having looked in every guide
For why he loved it best,
I've used up all its legends.
It won't say a word. Like him,
Who spent his last day on light and water.

IV

MOTHER CONJURING IN HONDO, TEXAS: 1945

Because she feels her husband in this breeze
Riffling her blouse and housedress,
She's outside in the early days of peace.
While the sun freckles her arms in Texas,
Rows of lights glow on the British airstrips,
And Americans drink tea brown as deerskin.
She forgives the Soho whores, conjuring instead
His high cheekbones and the whiff of Italy
He'll bring home, like autumn coming on.
Because her red hair and flammable skin
Can't take much sun, she yearns for him
To stand between her and dust storms.
Black widows spin webs beneath the sink.
My mother's ready to trade this poverty
For the bemedaled sparkle of his uniform
And after that, the double-breasted suits
He'll salvage from dry storage. How brashly
Sexual they'll feel against her chest. And so
She's stoical, a wife who pauses willingly,
Dustpan and brush in hand, on the back porch,
To watch the bombers pass over, until one
Dips its wings. And because she knows
His face best from underneath, she knows
What drove him home will send him out again —
First the manic squint, a quivering
In his deviated septum, then the vein
That pulses in his throat: that's when
This edginess in the midst of peace
Comes on like a crosswind, and he's gone.

AFTER BYPASS

The room, violet with iris and stasis, reeked
Those afternoons I sat with you; workers
In dustmasks thronged the skeletal girders
Just outside your window. Pouring concrete

Or crouched brooding over their blueprints,
They huddled and consulted like the doctors
We quizzed together, or I'd quiz as you slept.
Seasoned patients wobbled down the corridor,

Clutching red, heart-shaped pillows, inscribed
With the surgeon's autograph, and cross-
Sections of their reconstructed arteries,
All their lesions or occlusions cured.

Fresh from surgery, your sewn-up chest
Almost glowed through the sheer nightgown,
Its embossed ridge of stitches curving down
Between your breasts. What son could resist

A furtive look? When once you briefly woke
To my staring, I felt sure you'd recognized
That boy caught peeking through a dime-sized
Scratch in the whitewashed bathroom window

Thirty summers ago — an afternoon I took a dare
That left me exposed to you, breasts and hair
A white and dark ringing I couldn't name.
Today your yellowing catheter bag is gone,

And stabbing cries down the hall resound
Like a newborn. But it's pain
You wake to on this ward, and sutured wounds —
A husband dead, a son — no sedative can numb.

Opening your eyes to the son who's left,
Those workers, you say, *are perfect gentlemen.*
I take your arm, it's time for exercise; we join
The others, hugging those hearts to their chests.

AFTER THE MIRACLE

for Phil Edmondson

1.

I sit between you and your small son,
Shreds of wallpaper littering the living room,

Where unless a donor's found you're dying
Of a gene that's turned you lucent.

Zap! my nephew yells, *zap zap!*
Thumbing the remote of his Nintendo game,

He wastes each glowing enemy in his path.
The tubing forked around your head

Whispers you full of oxygen —
A hushed exhalation, like my own

Years ago, as I watched a mother wheel
Her scarred child through the supermarket,

Followed them really, stopping in their aisle
To stare, to remember; so now I *do* remember

The puckered holes he wheezed through,
The crusted sockets that contained his eyes,

And his single nailless finger raised,
Pointing at some cereal he'd seen on TV;

And as his mother pulled it from the shelf,
I turned away. Around the three of us,

Different shades of white paint streak
The walls, and patches of spackle shine

From brittle plaster, the underskin
Of a row house you bought for almost nothing.

Where my sister weeps in the kitchen,
Aimlessly tearing salad greens,

While you drift off in a medicated haze;
A house where certain words hurt to think of —

Livable, foundation, neighborhood;
A house in which there is no borderline

Between the punishing exactitude of memory
And the present rushing hell-bent

At our faces from the TV's glare,
As the respirator pants behind our backs,

My nephew Sam shouts *Zap!*
And a small boy whispers *I want that.*

2.

Once the rift in your flesh is sewn up
And the sinews begin to restitch;

As the subcutaneous fat shrinks from the trauma,
The capillaries reattach, and your blood

Flows without shunts;
After the tubes, withdrawn from your side,

No longer conduct the signals of pain
Muted now to irritation, and your wound

Loses its purplish hue, which gaped for a day
On the surgeon's table, an eyelid in shock;

And what's left is just this pentacle
Under your belt, and the regimen

Of medicines, supressing your body's code
To reject, then what can we know

Aside from our awed gossip on the phone,
Your good color, your firmer grip,

Your lapsed stare fading from memory,
Along with the dun-colored spots on your hands

Wiped clean as if by a washcloth?
Now that you've grown back your beard,

And roughly reborn to your age,
You stride up the path to your door

More quickly after you've been warned
A cold can thrive until it kills,

What does it feel like to walk
Into every moment unprotected?

Your jeans, looser now, chafe at the scar;
Your pores open to what pleases

Or infects; reawakened nerves send up
A new coolness as your sweat evaporates;

And across the roughness of your tongue,
There's a range from salt to sweet to lemony.

THE ACCIDENT

We wanted only to get home
Where the heat rises to a sudden
Dryness in the mouth: evidence
Of marriage on our breath. On the Turnpike,

Snow whipped its spindrift against the windshield,
Mounted on the guardrail, the median, and when
Our car slurred into its three-sixty reel,
Unwinding as a whiteness swaddled us,

Time didn't stop, speed, or slow,
So futureless was that single revolution.
For seconds we were hands on the clock's face,
The wheel in my grip, helpless play.

If our glances met, they witnessed nothing
Like recognition or requital, but
Our glances didn't meet. Then
With a shuddering punch to the bumper,

The guardrail set us straight:
No other cars in sight. No lights
In the woods. Even the snow immobile.
Till the engine caught, and we crept to the exit;

And turning over and over on the motel bed,
We fucked with the recklessness of the lucky,
The unhoused, the betrayed, our cries reaching
Only toward what's next, then next, then next.

THE BLACK MINUS

Remember the dark shriek
        That swooped into our room
                And punched us awake like a lungful
Of smoke? Only some crows outside,
        Though a few millennia ago
                We'd have called them omens,
Like those eagles from *The Odyssey*
        Strafing the mob of Ithakans,
                Which only old Halitherses
(*Keenest at reading birdflight*
        Into accurate speech) divines.
                On that morning of the crows,
Your test again turned up
        A black minus that means no.
                Soon the red net of your womb
Would crumble, your stomach grumbling
        As if from hunger, our disappointment
                A week-long stain. I confess
I can't grasp this cycle of loss
        As you do; I just can't see it
                As another soul snuffed out
Like the candle wick I extinguish
        With a thumb, forefinger, spit,
                After we make love, dispirited,
And doze off numb. For me,
        God's mainly superstition, and so
                Is this unnerving spirit
Our bodies keep sweating to conceive.
        We'd rather our labor were thoughtless,
                Like the evening I waltzed
With a neighbor's infant daughter —
        Her body immanent as rising dough
                In my grip, we swayed to the cool
Sound waves of Miles. I loved the vapor
        She breathed on my neck, and was
                Witness to that mystery,

As when I first saw you pray,
      How you bent one knee, by instinct,
            It seemed, and slid into the pew,
And how, throughout the service,
      Every time you knelt on cue,
            In bodily obedience
To what you couldn't see, my eyes
      Lowered against my will, as if
            The stone tiles stored miracles.
So maybe you know: were the crows
      That morning raw material? Later,
            When a mass of pigeons
Surged into an off-white uprush
      Outside my study window,
            Like ashes sucked through a flue,
I tried to get their whiteness right
      And failed, and threw away
            What wouldn't come to life,

And spent the morning looking at the sky.

NOCTURNE

Our eyes nearly shut, we hadn't planned
        To talk of death, when the word
                Itself, like a jolt

From the bedside phone, came crowding out
        Those idlings the childless
                Doze off with —

No name just right for our unconceived
        Daughter or son. Then I said
                Suppose one dies before

We die, its high-pitched syllable repeating,
        Ringing so true I could tell
                You heard it also,

Our hearts thumping through the bed frame
        Until there was no hope of sleep.
                Oh, we tried

To "talk the subject out,"
        Then to take deep breaths of it —
                Oxide we'll exhale

Someday for good; and today I'm up
        Working hard to tell you how
                I'm tired of this

Appetite for loss, every bereavement
        A kind of neighborhood I watch
                From my attic window,

Searching for lyric shocks to release
        Full-voiced odes and palinodes
                Wild as the ooze

Of bloodroot sap. This is the worst
Bad faith: insisting death requires
A body and a face

The way a heartbeat needs the name
Daniel, if it's a boy; *Angela*,
If it's a girl.

But even while I elegize our talk
(Hearing the neighbor's children
Smack a wiffle ball,

Then watching the smallest boy unleash
An insouciant arc of piss
Against his house),

I suspect the dead survive our praise
That shadows them, finally
To admonish us,

Like the night before my father died,
When I last listened to his voice —
Just thought I'd call.

I'm feeling much better; they say
I might go home this week or next —
And routinely erased

His message with the others on the tape.

FROM THE CORNER OF HIS EYE

Genesis 22

No, he never believed
It couldn't be wished again,
Especially when he watched
His father handle a knife —
Some long tooth or rib
From the charred bone-pile.
And each morning afterwards
Felt like that first morning
When saddling the beasts
The old man wouldn't look up;
Or the second morning
When they stopped for wood,
Strapping it on the animals,
The servants puzzled, silent;
Or the third morning
When lifting his head at last
His father only stared off
At the horizon's highest peak.
And on the fourth morning
They began the long hike up.

He'll never stop believing
Faith's a form of violence —
His wriggling hands bound
Behind his back, his father
Grasping the knife so tightly
The knuckles glowed through;
His small body writhing,
Instinctively disobedient;
The mingled stink of their sweat;
And then a hushed approach
From the corner of his eye:
The arm that pinned him there
Wrinkling, taking the white

Imprint of another's grip;
The sharp clang as the knife
Dropped; his cries echoing
That new, animal sound
Rumbling from a nearby bush . . .

Of course he can't forget
This willingness to sacrifice
What's loved to what is feared.
But this is not his worst
Conviction, though for years
He fled if a playmate grabbed
His wrist, recoiled from the rasp
Of firewood against his cheek,
Or woke nightly to the press
Of his own hands on his throat.
The worst surfaces later
When, a father now, he watches
From the corner of his eye
The maddening innocence of sons
At play, at sacrifice,
And suddenly recalls the act
Not as God's wish, not a test,
Not a father's faith but his desire.

THE FEEDER

If I prayed, I'd want to pray as Herbert prays in "Prayer" —
His figures lifting, like breezes in their restless inrush
Through a tree, to *Church-bels beyond the starres heard*
And finally to *something understood.* This morning,
Though, the planetree maple in my neighbor's yard,
Rankled and teased by the wind, makes a shushing sound,
As if to rebuke my wish. It's early May —
Pulling down screens I hear, over the neighborhood,
The wooden creak and metal stammer of repair: a roof reshingled,
Loosened fence posts dividing our untilled gardens
Nailed back into line, someone hauling lumber from his car,
Another scooping muck out of his gutters;
And when our neighbor Joe, the block's handyman,
Angles his truck into the narrow driveway next door
Then spreads his dropcloth on the porch,
I know without having to look: he'll paint the ceiling
Blue to match the sky. Wasn't it last spring
Joe's wife Margaret rang our doorbell
With flowers left over from her sister's funeral?
Peonies, carnations, yellow and white daisies,
Even, incongruously, a showy bird-of-paradise,
All fanned out in a plastic tub, the water
Sloshing on our steps, her shoes. The week before,
I'd driven by the ambulance double-parked at their address,
Watched the paramedics wheel the stretcher in,
Then ducked into my house, in order not to see the body
Gurneyed to the curbside like something repossessed.
We still have that tub, it's under the sink,
As if she'd told us *keep it, I've got dozens like it,*
And maybe she does. Who wouldn't want to borrow
Some of the amplitude that brought her to our door?
Who wouldn't wish for eyes that don't by habit look away?
When my brother had been dead about a year,
We brought the feeder he gave us up from the basement
Where it moldered in a scree of cement dust. No birds

At first, through March and April. Then
The seed-level lowered visibly,
Which could have been the wind, then sparrows
Browsed on its perch. Careful not to get too close,
We've let them come and go in the corner of our eyes,
The way couples who are learning how to mourn
Wake to their losses — sidelong and glancing:
The sky's a chill blue; the maple, perturbed,
Shakes sunlight down through its crown.
God's breath in man returning to his birth,
The soul in paraphrase, heart in pilgrimage . . .
Leaning out the window now, I measure
More seed into the feeder, one hand holding it steady,
The other pouring carefully from the sack
But not too carefully, knowing whatever spills
The birds will also come across and eat.